EGYPTIAN TALES

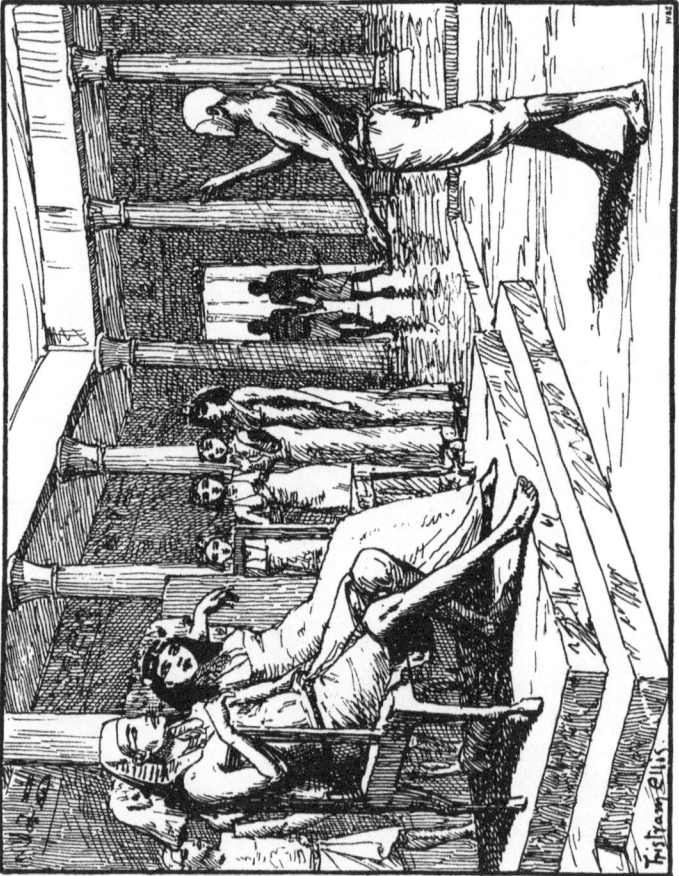

EGYPTIAN TALES

TRANSLATED FROM THE PAPYRI

FIRST SERIES

IVth TO XIIth DYNASTY

EDITED BY

W. M. FLINDERS PETRIE, Hon. D.C.L.

EDWARDS PROFESSOR OF EGYPTOLOGY, UNIVERSITY
COLLEGE, LONDON

ILLUSTRATED BY TRISTRAM ELLIS

METHUEN & CO.
36 ESSEX STREET, STRAND
LONDON
1895

CONTENTS

LIST OF ILLUSTRATIONS

INTRODUCTION

IT is strange that while literature occupies
so much attention as at present, and
while fiction is the largest division of our
book-work, the oldest literature and fiction
of the world should yet have remained
unpresented to English readers. The tales
of ancient Egypt have appeared collectively
only in French, in the charming volume
of Maspero's "Contes Populaires"; while
some have been translated into English at
scattered times in volumes of the "Records
of the Past." But research moves forward;
and translations that were excellent twenty
years ago may now be largely improved, as
we attain more insight into the language.

For another reason also there is a wide
ground for the present volume.   In no case
have any illustrations been attempted, to give
that basis for imagination which is all the
more needed when reading of an age and
a land unfamiliar to our ideas.   When
following a narrative, whether of real events
or of fiction, many persons—perhaps most—
find themselves unconsciously framing in
their minds the scenery and the beings of
which they are reading.   To give a correct
picture of the character of each of the various
ages to which these tales belong, has been
the aim of the present illustrations.   A
definite period has been assigned to each tale,
in accordance with the indications, or the
history, involved in it ; and, so far as our
present knowledge goes, all the details of life
in the scenes here illustrated are rendered in
accord with the period of the story.

To some purely scholastic minds it may
seem presumptuous to intermingle translations of notable documents with fanciful

illustrations. But, considering the greater
precision with which in recent years we have
been able to learn the changes and the
fashions of ancient life in Egypt, and the
essentially unhistorical nature of most of
these tales, there seems ample reason to
provide such material for the reader's
imagination in following the stories; it may
give them more life and reality, and may
emphasise the differences which existed
between the different periods to which these
tales refer.

It will be noticed how the growth of the
novel is shadowed out in the varied grounds
and treatment of the tales. The earliest is
purely a collection of marvels or fabulous
incidents of the simplest kind. Then we
advance to contrasts between town and
country, between Egypt and foreign lands.
Then personal adventure, and the interest in
schemes and successes, becomes the staple
material; while only in the later periods does
character come in as the groundwork. The

same may be seen in English literature—
first the tales of wonders and strange lands,
then the novel of adventure, and lastly the
novel of character.

In translating these documents into English
I have freely used the various translations
already published in other languages; but in
all cases more or less revision and retransla-
tion from the original has been made. In
this matter I am indebted to Mr. F. Ll.
Griffith, who has in some cases—as in Anpu
and Bata—almost entirely retranslated the
original papyrus. The material followed in
each instance will be found stated in the
notes accompanying the tales. As to the
actual phraseology, I am alone responsible
for that. How far original idiom should be
retained in any translation is always a debated
question, and must entirely depend on the
object in view. Here the purpose of render-
ing the work intelligible to ordinary readers
required the modifying of some idioms and
the paraphrasing of others. But so far

as possible the style and tone of the original has been preserved, and whatever could be easily followed has been left to speak for itself. In many plainnesses of speech the old Egyptian resembled the modern Oriental, or our own forefathers, more than ourselves in this age of squeamishness as yet unparalleled in the world. To avoid offence a few little modifications of words have been made ; but rather than give a false impression by tampering with any of the narrative, I have omitted the sequel of the last tale and given only an outline of it. The diction adopted has been the oldest that could be used without affectation when dealing with the early times. It has been purposely modified in the later tales ; and in the last —which is of Ptolemaic authorship — a modern style has been followed as more compatible with the later tone of the narrative.

For the illustrations Mr. Tristram Ellis's familiarity with Egypt has been of good

account in his life-like scenes here used.
For each drawing I have searched for the
material among the monuments and remains
of the age in question. The details of the
dresses, the architecture, and the utensils,
are all in accord with the period of each
tale.   In the tale of Setnau two different
styles are introduced. Ahura is probably
of the time of Amenhotep III., whereas
Setnau is a son of Ramessu II.; and the
change of fashion between the two different
dynasties has been followed as distinctive of
the two persons, one a *ka* or double of the
deceased, the other a living man. To the
reader who starts with the current idea that
all Egyptians were alike, this continual
change from one period to another may seem
almost fanciful.   But it rests on such certain
authority that we may hope that this little
volume may have its use as an object-lesson
in practical archæology.

The use and abuse of notes is a matter of
dispute.   To be constantly interrupted in

reading by some needless and elementary explanation is an impertinence both to the author and the reader : the one cannot resent it, the other therefore resents it for both. But what is to be deemed needless entirely depends on the reader : I have been asked in what country Pompei is, as it is not in the English Gazetteer. Rather than intrude, then, on the reader when he is in high discourse with the ancients, I humbly set up my interpreter's booth next door ; and if he cares to call in, and ask about any difficulties, I shall be glad to help him if I can. Not even numbers are intruded to refer to notes ; for how often an eager reader has been led off his trail, and turned blithely to refer to 37 or 186 only to find, " See J. Z. xxxviii. 377," at which he gnashed his teeth and cursed such interruptions. So those to whom the original tales are obscure are humbly requested to try for some profit from the remarks after them, that have been gleaned by the translator.

Much might be said by a " folk-lorist "—in proportion to his ardour. But as there are folk-lorists and folk--lorists, and the schools of Rabbi Andrew and Rabbi Joseph write different targums, I have left each to make his own commentary without prejudice.

TALES OF THE MAGICIANS

ONE day, when King Khufu reigned over all the land, he said to his chancellor, who stood before him, "Go call me my sons and my councillors, that I may ask of them a thing." And his sons and his councillors came and stood before him, and he said to them, "Know ye a man who can tell me tales of the deeds of the magicians?"

Then the royal son Khafra stood forth and said, "I will tell thy majesty a tale of the days of thy forefather Nebka, the blessed; of what came to pass when he went into the temple of Ptah of Ankhtaui."

9

KHAFRA'S TALE

" His majesty was walking unto the temple of Ptah, and went unto the house of the chief reciter Uba-aner, with his train. Now when the wife of Uba-aner saw a page, among those who stood behind the king, her heart longed after him ; and she sent her servant unto him, with a present of a box full of garments.

" And he came then with the servant. Now there was a lodge in the garden of Uba-aner ; and one day the page said to the wife of Uba-aner, ' In the garden of Uba-aner there is now a lodge ; behold, let us therein take our pleasure.' So the wife of Uba-aner sent to the steward who had charge over the garden, saying, ' Let the lodge which is in the garden be made ready.' And she remained there, and rested and drank with the page until the sun went down.

" And when the even was now come the

page went forth to bathe. And the steward
said, 'I must go and tell Uba-aner of this
matter.' Now when this day was past, and
another day came, then went the steward to
Uba-aner, and told him of all these things.

"Then said Uba-aner, 'Bring me my casket
of ebony and electrum.' And they brought
it; and he fashioned a crocodile of wax,
seven fingers long : and he enchanted it,
and said, 'When the page comes and bathes
in my lake, seize on him.' And he gave
it to the steward, and said to him, 'When
the page shall go down into the lake to
bathe, as he is daily wont to do, then throw
in this crocodile behind him.' And the
steward went forth bearing the crocodile.

"And the wife of Uba-aner sent to the
steward who had charge over the garden,
saying, 'Let the lodge which is in the garden
be made ready, for I come to tarry there.'

"And the lodge was prepared with all
good things ; and she came and made merry
therein with the page. And when the even

was now come, the page went forth to bathe as he was wont to do. And the steward cast in the wax crocodile after him into the water; and, behold! it became a great crocodile seven cubits in length, and it seized on the page.

"And Uba-aner abode yet seven days with the king of Upper and Lower Egypt, Nebka, the blessed, while the page was stifled in the crocodile. And after the seven days were passed, the king of Upper and Lower Egypt, Nebka, the blessed, went forth, and Uba-aner went before him.

"And Uba-aner said unto his majesty, 'Will your majesty come and see this wonder that has come to pass in your days unto a page?' And the king went with Uba-aner. And Uba-aner called unto the crocodile and said, 'Bring forth the page.' And the crocodile came forth from the lake with the page. Uba-aner said unto the king, 'Behold, whatever I command this crocodile he will do it.' And his majesty said, 'I pray you send back

THE STEWARD AND THE WAX CROCODILE

this crocodile.' And Uba-aner stooped and took up the crocodile, and it became in his hand a crocodile of wax. And then Uba-aner told the king that which had passed in his house with the page and his wife. And his majesty said unto the crocodile, ' Take to thee thy prey.' And the crocodile plunged into the lake with his prey, and no man knew whither he went.

" And his majesty the king of Upper and Lower Egypt, Nebka, the blessed, commanded, and they brought forth the wife of Uba-aner to the north side of the harem, and burnt her with fire, and cast her ashes in the river

" This is a wonder that came to pass in the days of thy forefather the king of Upper and Lower Egypt, Nebka, of the acts of the chief reciter Uba-aner."

His majesty the king of Upper and Lower Egypt, Khufu, then said, " Let there be presented to the king Nebka, the blessed, a thousand loaves, a hundred draughts of beer,

an ox, two jars of incense ; and let there
be presented a loaf, a jar of beer, a jar of
incense, and a piece of meat to the chief
reciter Uba-aner ; for I have seen the token
of his learning." And they did all things as
his majesty commanded.

BAUFRA'S TALE

The royal son Bau-f-ra then stood forth
and spake. He said, " I will tell thy majesty
of a wonder which came to pass in the days
of thy father Seneferu, the blessed, of the
deeds of the chief reciter Zazamankh. One
day King Seneferu, being weary, went
throughout his palace seeking for a pleasure
to lighten his heart, but he found none.
And he said, ' Haste, and bring before me
the chief reciter and scribe of the rolls
Zazamankh' ; and they straightway brought
him. And the king said, ' I have sought in
my palace for some delight, but I have found
none.' Then said Zazamankh to him, ' Let

thy majesty go upon the lake of the palace, and let there be made ready a boat, with all the fair maidens of the harem of thy palace; and the heart of thy majesty shall be re- freshed with the sight, in seeing their rowing up and down the water, and seeing the goodly pools of the birds upon the lake, and beholding its sweet fields and grassy shores; thus will thy heart be lightened. And I also will go with thee. Bring me twenty oars of ebony, inlayed with gold, with blades of light wood, inlayed with electrum; and bring me twenty maidens, fair in their limbs, their bosoms and their hair, all virgins; and bring me twenty nets, and give these nets unto the maidens for their garments.' And they did according to all the commands of his majesty.

"And they rowed down the stream and up the stream, and the heart of his majesty was glad with the sight of their rowing. But one of them at the steering struck her hair, and her jewel of new malachite fell

3

into the water. And she ceased her song,
and rowed not ; and her companions ceased,
and rowed not.   And his majesty said,
' Row you not further ? '   And they replied,
' Our little steerer here stays and rows not.'
His majesty then said to her, ' Wherefore
rowest thou not? ' She replied, ' It is for
my jewel of new malachite which is fallen
in the water.'   And he said to her, ' Row
on, for behold I will replace it.'   And she
answered, ' But I want my own piece back
in its setting.'   And his majesty said, 'Haste,
bring me the chief reciter Zazamankh,' and
they brought him.   And his majesty said,
    Zazamankh, my brother, I have done as
thou sayedst, and the heart of his majesty
is refreshed with the sight of their rowing.
But now a jewel of new malachite of one of
the little ones is fallen in the water, and she
ceases and rows not, and she has spoilt the
rowing of her side.   And I said to her,
" Wherefore rowest thou not ? " and she
answered to me, " It is for my jewel of new

ZAZAMANKH FINDING THE JEWEL

malachite which is fallen in the water." I
replied to her, " Row on, for behold I will
replace it " ; and she answered to me, " But
I want my own piece again back in its
setting." ' Then the chief reciter Zazamankh
spake his magic speech. And he placed one
part of the waters of the lake upon the
other, and discovered the jewel lying upon
a shard ; and he took it up and gave it unto
its mistress. And the water, which was
twelve cubits deep in the middle, reached
now to twenty-four cubits after he turned it.
And he spake, and used his magic speech ;
and he brought again the water of the lake
to its place. And his majesty spent a joyful
day with the whole of the royal house.
Then rewarded he the chief reciter Zazamankh with all good things. Behold, this
is a wonder that came to pass in the days of
thy father, the king of Upper and Lower
Egypt, Seneferu, of the deeds of the chief
reciter, the scribe of the rolls, Zazamankh."

Then said the majesty of the king of

Upper and Lower Egypt, Khufu, the blessed, " Let there be presented an offering of a thousand cakes, one hundred draughts of beer, an ox, and two jars of incense to the king of Upper and Lower Egypt, Seneferu, the blessed ; and let there be given a loaf, a jar of beer, and a jar of incense to the chief reciter, the scribe of the rolls, Zazamankh ; for I have seen the token of his learning." And they did all things as his majesty commanded.

HORDEDEF'S TALE

THE royal son Hordedef then stood forth and spake. He said, " Hitherto hast thou only heard tokens of those who have gone before, and of which no man knoweth their truth. But I will show thy majesty a man of thine own days." And his majesty said, " Who is he, Hordedef?" And the royal son Hordedef answered, " It is a certain man named Dedi, who dwells at Ded-

HORDEDEF LEADING DEDI TO THE SHIP

sneferu. He is a man of one hundred and
ten years old; and he eats five hundred
loaves of bread, and a side of beef, and
drinks one hundred draughts of beer, unto
this day. He knows how to restore the
head that is smitten off; he knows how to
cause the lion to follow him trailing his
halter on the ground; he knows the
designs of the dwelling of Tahuti. The
majesty of the king of Upper and Lower
Egypt, Khufu, the blessed, has long sought
for the designs of the dwelling of Tahuti,
that he may make the like of them in his
pyramid."

And his majesty said, "Thou, thyself,
Hordedef, my son, bring him to me." Then
were the ships made ready for the king's
son Hordedef, and he went up the stream
to Dedsneferu. And when the ships had
moored at the haven, he landed, and sat
him in a litter of ebony, the poles of which
were of cedar wood overlayed with gold.
Now when he drew near to Dedi, they set

down the litter.   And he arose to greet
Dedi, and found him lying on a palmstick
couch at the door of his house ; one servant
held his head and rubbed him, and another
rubbed his feet.

And the king's son Hordedef said,
" Thy state is that of one who lives to
good old age ; for old age is the end of
our voyage, the time of embalming, the
time of burial.   Lie, then, in the sun, free
of infirmities, without the babble of dotage :
this is the salutation to worthy age.   I come
from far to call thee, with a message from
my father Khufu, the blessed, for thou
shalt eat of the best which the king gives,
and of the food which those have who follow
after him ; that he may bring thee in good
estate to thy fathers who are in the tomb."

And Dedi replied to him, " Peace to thee !
Peace to thee !   Hordedef, son of the king,
beloved of his father.   May thy father Khufu,
the blessed, praise thee, may he advance
thee amongst the elders, may thy *ka* prevail

against the enemy, may thy soul know the
right road to the gate of him who clothes
the afflicted ; this is the salutation to the
king's son." Then the king's son, Hordedef,
stretched forth his hands to him, and raised
him up, and went with him to the haven,
giving unto him his arm. Then said Dedi,
" Let there be given me a boat, to bring me
my youths and my books." And they made
ready for him two boats with their rowers.
And Dedi went down the river in the barge
in which was the king's son Hordedef.
And when he had reached the palace, the
king's son, Hordedef, entered in to give
account unto his majesty the king of Upper
and Lower Egypt, Khufu, the blessed.
Then said the king's son Hordedef, "O
king, life, wealth, and health ! My lord,
I have brought Dedi." His majesty replied,
" Bring him to me speedily." And his
majesty went into the hall of columns of
Pharaoh (life, wealth, and health), and
Dedi was led before him. And his majesty

said, "Wherefore is it, Dedi, that I have not
yet seen thee?" And Dedi answered, "He
who is called it is that comes; the king
(life, wealth, and health) calls me, and
behold I come." And his majesty said,
"Is it true, that which men say, that thou
canst restore the head which is smitten off?"
And Dedi replied, "Truly, I know that, O
king (life, wealth, and health), my lord."
And his majesty said, "Let one bring me a
prisoner who is in prison, that his punishment
may be fulfilled." And Dedi said, "Let it
not be a man, O king, my lord; behold
we do not even thus to our cattle." And a
duck was brought unto him, and its head
was cut off. And the duck was laid on the
west side of the hall, and its head on the east
side of the hall. And Dedi spake his magic
speech. And the duck fluttered along the
ground, and its head came likewise; and
when it had come part to part the duck
stood and quacked. And they brought
likewise a goose before him, and he did

DEDI ENCHANTING THE DUCK

even so unto it. His majesty caused an
ox to be brought, and its head cast on the
ground. And Dedi spake his magic speech.
And the ox stood upright behind him, and
followed him with his halter trailing on the
ground.

And King Khufu said, " And is it true
what is said, that thou knowest the number
of the designs of the dwelling of Tahuti ? "
And Dedi replied, " Pardon me, I know not
their number, O king (life, wealth, and
health), but I know where they are." And
his majesty said, " Where is that ? " And
Dedi replied, " There is a chest of whetstone
in a chamber named the plan-room, in Heliopolis ; they are in this chest." And Dedi
said further unto him, " O king (life,
wealth, and health), my lord, it is no It
that is to bring them to thee." And his
majesty said, " Who, then, is it that shall
bring them to me ? " And Dedi answered
to him, " It is the eldest of the three children who are in the body of Rud-didet who

shall bring them to thee." And his majesty said, " Would that it may be as thou sayest ! And who is this Rud-didet ? " And Dedi replied, "She is the wife of a priest of Ra, lord of Sakhebu. And she has conceived these three sons by Ra, lord of Sakhebu, and the god has promised her that they shall fulfil this noble office (of reigning) over all this land, and that the eldest of them shall be high priest in Heliopolis." And his majesty's heart became troubled for this; but Dedi spake unto him, " What is this that thou thinkest, O king (life, wealth, health), my lord? Is it because of these three children ? I tell thee thy son shall reign, and thy son's son, and then one of them." His majesty said, " And when shall Rud-didet bear these ? " And he replied, "She shall bear them on the 25th of the month Tybi." And his majesty said, " When the banks of the canal of Letopolis are cut, I will walk there that I may see the temple of Ra, lord of Sakhebu." And

Dedi replied, " Then I will cause that there be four cubits of water by the banks of the canal of Letopolis." When his majesty returned to his palace, his majesty said, " Let them place Dedi in the house of the royal son Hordedef, that he may dwell with him, and let them give him a daily portion of a thousand loaves, a hundred draughts of beer, an ox, and a hundred bunches of onions." And they did everything as his majesty commanded.

And one day it came to pass that Ruddidet felt the pains of birth. And the majesty of Ra, lord of Sakhebu, said unto Isis, to Nebhat, to Meskhent, to Hakt, and to Khnumu, " Go ye, and deliver Ruddidet of these three children that she shall bear, who are to fulfil this noble office over all this land ; that they may build up your temples, furnish your altars with offerings, supply your tables of libation, and increase your endowments." Then went these deities ; their fashion they made as that of dancing-

4

girls, and Khnumu was with them as a porter. They drew near unto the house of Ra-user, and found him standing, with his girdle fallen. And they played before him with their instruments of music. But he said unto them, " My ladies, behold, here is a woman who feels the pains of birth." They said to him, " Let us see her, for we know how to help her." And he replied, " Come, then." And they entered in straight-way to Rud-didet, and they closed the door on her and on themselves. Then Isis stood before her, and Nebhat stood behind her, and Hakt helped her. And Isis said, " O child, by thy name of User-ref, do not do violence." And the child came upon her hands, as a child of a cubit ; its bones were strong, the beauty of its limbs was like gold, and its hair was like true lapis lazuli. They washed him, and prepared him, and placed him on a carpet on the brickwork. Then Meskhent approached him and said, " This is a king who shall

THE GODDESSES AND KHNUMU COMING TO RA-USER

reign over all the land." And Khnumu gave
strength to his limbs. Then Isis stood
before her, and Nebhat stood behind her,
and Hakt helped her. And Isis said, " O
child, by thy name of Sah-ra, stay not in
her." Then the child came upon her hands,
a child of a cubit ; its bones were strong,
the beauty of its limbs was like gold,
and its hair was like true lapis lazuli. They
washed him, and prepared him, and layed
him on a carpet on the brickwork. Then
Meskhent approached him and said, " This
is a king who shall reign over all the land."
And Khnumu gave strength to his limbs.
Then Isis stood before her, and Nebhat stood
behind her, and Hakt helped her. And Isis
said, " O child, by thy name of Kaku,
remain not in darkness in her." And the
child came upon her hands, a child of a
cubit ; its bones were strong, the beauty of
its limbs was like gold, and its hair was
like true lapis lazuli. And Meskhent approached him and said, " This is a king who

shall reign over all the land." And Khnumu gave strength to his limbs. And they washed him, and prepared him, and layed him on a carpet on the brickwork.

And the deities went out, having delivered Rud-didet of the three children. And they said, " Rejoice ! O Ra-user, for behold three children are born unto thee." And he said unto them, " My ladies, and what shall I give unto ye? Behold, give this bushel of barley here unto your porter, that ye may take it as your reward to the brew-house." And Khnumu loaded himself with the bushel of barley. And they went away toward the place from which they came. And Isis spake unto these goddesses, and said, " Wherefore have we come without doing a marvel for these children, that we may tell it to their father who has sent us ? " Then made they the divine diadems of the king (life, wealth, and health), and laid them in the bushel of barley. And they caused the clouds to come with wind and

THE GODDESSES HIDING THE CROWN

rain ; and they turned back again unto the house. And they said, "Let us put this barley in a closed chamber, sealed up, until . we return northward, dancing." And they placed the barley in a close chamber.

And Rud-didet purified herself, with a purification of fourteen days. And she said to her handmaid, "Is the house made ready?" And she replied, "All things are made ready, but the brewing barley is not yet brought." And Rud-didet said, "Wherefore is the brewing barley not yet brought?" And the servant answered, "It would all of it long since be ready if the barley had not been given to the dancing-girls, and lay in the chamber under their seal." Rud-didet said, "Go down, and bring of it, and Ra-user shall give them in its stead when he shall come." And the handmaid went, and opened the chamber. And she heard talking and singing, music and dancing, quavering, and all things which are performed for a king in his chamber. And she returned and told to

Rud-didet all that she had heard. And she went through the chamber, but she found not the place where the sound was. And she layed her temple to the sack, and found that the sounds were in it. She placed it in a chest, and put that in another locker, and tied it fast with leather, and layed it in the store-room, where the things were, and sealed it. And Ra-user came returning from the field ; and Rud-didet repeated unto him these things ; and his heart was glad above all things ; and they sat down and made a joyful day.

And after these days it came to pass that Rud-didet was wroth with her servant, and beat her with stripes. And the servant said unto those that were in the house, " Shall it be done thus unto me ? She has borne three kings, and I will go and tell this to his majesty King Khufu the blessed." And she went, and found the eldest brother of her mother, who was binding his flax on the floor. And he said to

THE HANDMAID LISTENING TO THE FESTIVITY

her, "Whither goest thou, my little maid?"
And she told him of all these things. And
her brother said to her, "Wherefore comest
thou thus to me? Shall I agree to trea-
chery?" And he took a bunch of the flax
to her, and laid on her a violent blow. And
the servant went to fetch a handful of water,
and a crocodile carried her away.

Her uncle went therefore to tell of this
to Rud-didet; and he found Rud-didet
sitting, her head on her knees, and her
heart beyond measure sad. And he said to
her, "My lady, why makest thou thy heart
thus?" And she answered, "It is because of
this little wretch that was in the house;
behold she went out saying, 'I will go and
tell it.'" And he bowed his head unto the
ground, and said, "My lady, she came and
told me of these things, and made her complaint unto me; and I laid on her a violent
blow. And she went forth to draw water,
and a crocodile carried her away."

(*The rest of the tale is lost.*)

REMARKS

The tales of the magicians are only preserved in a single copy, and of that the beginning is entirely lost. The papyrus was brought
from Egypt by an English traveller, and was
purchased by the Berlin Museum from the
property of Lepsius, who had received it
from the owner, Miss Westcar : hence it is
known as the Westcar papyrus. It was
written probably in the XIIth Dynasty, but
doubtless embodied tales, which had been
floating for generations before, about the
names of the early kings. It shows us
probably the kind of material that existed
for the great recension of the pre-monu-
mental history, made in the time of Seti I.
Those ages of the first three dynasties were
as long before that recension as we are after
it ; and this must always be remembered in
considering the authority of the Egyptian
records.

This papyrus has been more thoroughly

studied than most, perhaps more than any
other. Erman has devoted two volumes to
it; publishing the whole in photographic
facsimile, transcribed in hieroglyphs, transcribed in the modern alphabet, translated
literally, translated freely, commented on
and discussed word by word, and with a
complete glossary of all words used in it.
This exhaustive publication is named " Der
Märchen des Papyrus Westcar." Moreover,
Maspero has given a current translation in
the " Contes Populaires," 2nd edit. pp.
53–86.

The scheme of these tales is that they
are all told to King Khufu by his sons;
and as the beginning is lost, eight lines
are here added to explain this and introduce
the subject. The actual papyrus begins
with the last few words of a previous
tale concerning some other magician under
an earlier king. Then comes the tale of
Khafra, next that of Bau-f-ra, and lastly
that of Hor.dedef.

It need hardly be said that these tales are quite fictitious. The king and his successor Khafra are real, but the other sons cannot be identified ; and the confusion of supposing three kings of the Vth Dynasty to be triplets born early in the IVth Dynasty, shows what very vague ideas of their own history the Egyptians had when these tales were formed. This does not prevent our seeing that they embodied some very important traditions, and gives us an unequalled picture of the early civilisation.

In the earliest tale of the three there seems at first sight merely a sketch of faithlessness and revenge. But **Page 10.** there is probably much more in it. To read it aright we must bear in mind the position of woman in ancient Egypt. If, in later ages, Islam has gone to the extreme of the man determining

his own divorce at a word, in early
times almost the opposite system pre-
vailed. All property belonged to the
woman ; all that a man could earn, or
inherit, was made over to his wife ; and
families always reckoned back further on
the mother's side than the father's. As
the changes in historical times have been
in the direction of men's rights, it is
very unlikely that this system of female
predominance was invented or introduced,
but rather that it descends from primitive
times. In this tale we see, then, at the
beginning of our knowledge of the country,
the clashing of two different social systems.
The reciter is strong for men's rights, he
brings destruction on the wife, and never
even gives her name, but always calls her
merely " the wife of Uba-aner." But
behind all this there is probably the
remains of a very different system. The
servant employed by the mistress seems
to see nothing outrageous in her proceed-

ings ; and even the steward, who is on
the master's side, waits a day or two
before reporting matters.   When we re-
member the supremacy in property and
descent which women held in Egypt, and
then read this tale, it seems that it
belongs to the close of a social system
like that of the Nairs, in which the lady
makes her selection—with variations from
time to time.   The incident of sending a
present of clothing is curiously like the
tale about a certain English envoy, whose
proprieties were sadly ruffled in the Nair
country, when a lady sent him a grand
shawl with an intimation of her choice.
The priestesses of Amen retained to the
last this privilege of choice, as being
under divine, and not human protection ;
but it seems to have become unseemly in
late times.

The hinging of this tale, and of those
that follow it, upon the use of magic,
shows how thoroughly the belief in magic

powers was ingrained in the Egyptians. Now such a belief implies the presence of magicians, and shows how familiar must have been the claim to such powers, and the practising of the tricks of witchcraft, so prevalent in Africa in modern times. The efficacy of a model, such as this crocodile of wax, is an idea continually met with in Egypt. The system of tomb furniture and decoration, of *ka* statues, of *ushabtis* or figures to work for the deceased, and the models placed in foundation deposits, all show how a model was supposed to have the efficacy of an actual reality. Even in the latest tale of all (written in Ptolemaic times), Setnau makes a model of a boat and men, to be sunk in the river to work for him. The reconversion of the crocodile to wax, on being taken up by the magician, reminds us of the serpent becoming again a rod when taken up by Aaron.

The punishment of burning alive is very

rarely, if ever, mentioned in Egyptian history, though it occurs in modern Egyptian tales : and it looks as if it were brought in here rather as a dire horror for the climax than as a probable incident. The place of the penalty, in front of the harem, or the private portion of the palace, was evidently for the intimidation of other ladies.

At the close of each tale, King ¡Khufu, to whom it is told, orders funerary offerings by the usual formula, to be presented in honour of the king under whom the wonder took place. On the tablets of the tombs in the early times, there is usually recorded the offering— or, rather, the pious desire that there should be offered—thousands of loaves, of oxen, of gazelles, of cranes, &c., for a deceased person. Such expression cost no more by the thousand than by the dozen, so thousands came to be the usual expression in all ordaining of offerings.

We are so accustomed to think of
tedium as something modern, that it seems
strange to find in the oldest tales
Page 16. in the world how the first king
of whom we know anything was bored
by his pleasures. A reward for discover-
ing a new pleasure is the very basis of
the tale of Sneferu ; and the wise man's
remedy of a day in the country is still
the best resource, though all that we
know as human history has tried its
experiments in enjoyment since then. The
flavour of the ballet thrown in, by the
introduction of the damsels of the household clad in fishing nets, is not yet
obsolete in modern amusements ; and even
in this century Muhammed Ali had resource
to the same way of killing time, as he
was rowed about by his *harem*, but on
an artificial lake.

The use of two large oars for steering
explains the detail of the story. The oars
were one on each side of the stern, and

were each managed by a steerer.   From the
tale we see that the steerer led the song of
the rowers, and if the leader ceased, all that
side of the boat ceased also.   The position
of the lost jewel upon the hair shows that
it was in a fillet set with inlaying, like that
seen on early figures, such as Nefert at
Medum, who wears a fillet of rosettes to
retain the hair ; and the position of the
steering oar attached to a post, with the
handle rising high in the air, explains how it
could strike the fillet and displace the jewel.

The last tale is really double, a tale within
a tale.   It begins with the wonders done by
Page 22.   Dedi, and then goes on with the
history of the children about whom
he prophesied to Khufu.

The village of Dedi was probably near
Medum, as in the temple of Sneferu at
Medum an offering was found presented by
a worshipper to the gods of Ded-sneferu :

hence the background which is here given for the scene of Hordedef leading old Dedi. The translation of "the designs of the dwelling of Tahuti" is not certain ; but the passage seems to refer to some architectural plan which was desired for the pyramid.

The story of Rud-didet is remarkable historically. She is said to be wife of the priest of Ra, her children are sons of Ra, and they are the first three kings of the Vth dynasty, and supplanted the line of Khufu. This points to the Vth Dynasty having been a priestly usurpation ; and on looking at its history we see two confirmations of this. The title " Son of Ra " is so common in most ages in Egypt that it is taken for granted, and is applied in lists to any second cartouche ; but it is not found until well into the Vth Dynasty ; the earlier kings were not descendants of Ra, and it is only on arriving at this dynasty, which claimed descent from Ra, through the wife

of the priest of Ra, that we find the claim
of each king to be a " son of Ra." Another
confirmation of this priestly descent is the
abundance of priesthoods established for the
kings of the Vth Dynasty ; a care which
agrees with their having a priestly origin ;
while in the tale it is particularly said that
they would build up the temples, furnish
the altars with offerings, supply the tables
of libations, and increase the religious endowments.

The names of the three children are a
play upon the names of the first three kings
of the Vth Dynasty. User-kaf is made into
User-ref ; Sahu-ra is written Sah-ra ; and
Kaka is Kaku ; thus making allusions to
their births. The comparison of the hair
to true lapis lazuli seems very strange ; but
there is often a confusion between black
and blue in uneducated races, and *azrak*
means either dark blue or green, or black, at
present in Arabic. Lapis lazuli is brought
in to the name of the queen of Ramessu

VI., who was called "gold and lazuli," *Nub-khesdeb* ; recalling the comparison here of personal beauty to these precious materials.

It is noticeable here that in a tale of the Vth Dynasty, certainly written as early as the XIIth Dynasty, we find professional dancers commonly recognised, and going on travels through the country, with a porter.

From this tale we also learn that Egyptian women underwent a purification of fourteen days, during which they kept apart and did not attend to any household matters. The mistress of the house here inquires if the preparations are made for the feast on her return to household affairs ; and hears then how the beer cannot be made for lack of the barley.

The securing of the sack is just in accord with the remains of this early period ; the use of boxes, of thongs of leather for tying and of clay sealings for securing property, were all familiar matters in the XIIth Dynasty, as we learn from Kahun.

The present close of the tale is evidently only a stage in it, when the treacherous maid meets with the common doom of the wicked in Egyptian romance. How it was continued is a matter of speculation, but Khufu ought certainly to reappear and to order great rewards for Dedi, who up to this has only had maintenance on his requisite scale provided for him. Yet it is imperative that the children shall be saved from his wrath, as they are the kings of the Vth Dynasty. There may be a long episode lost of their flight and adventures.

One reference to a date needs notice. The 25th of the month Tybi is said to be the predicted birthday of the children; and Khufu refers to going to Sakhebu about that time apparently, when the banks of the canal are cut and the land was drying after the inundation, whereon Dedi threatens that the water shall still be deep there. This points to 25th Tybi being about the close of the inundation. This would be about

the case both in the beginning of the IVth
Dynasty, and also in the XIIth Dynasty,
when the papyrus was perhaps written : hence
there is nothing conclusive to be drawn from
this allusion so far. But when we compare
this tale with those following, we see good
ground for its belonging to a time before
the XIIth Dynasty. The following tale of
the peasant and the workman evidently
belongs to the IXth or Xth Dynasties, when
Herakleopolis was the capital, and Sanehat
is certainly of the XIIth Dynasty. Yet in
those we see character and incident made the
basis of interest, in place of the childish
profusion of marvels of the Tales of the
Magicians. It seems impossible not to suppose that they belong to very different ages
and canons of taste ; and hence we cannot
refer the crudities of the Khufu tales to the
time of the far more elaborate and polished
recital of the adventures of Sanehat in the
XIIth Dynasty. Being thus obliged to
suppose an earlier date for these tales, the

allusion to the month Tybi throws us back
to a very early period—the IVth Dynasty
—for their original outlines.   Doubtless they
were modified by reciters, and probably took
shape in the Vth or VIth Dynasties ; but
yet we must regard them as belonging
practically to the age to which they refer.

IXth DYNASTY

THE PEASANT AND THE WORKMAN

THERE dwelt in the Sekhet Hemat—
or salt country—a peasant called the
Sekhti, with his wife and children, his asses
and his dogs; and he trafficked in all good
things of the Sekhet Hemat to Henenseten.
Behold now he went] with rushes, natron, and
salt, with wood and pods, with stones and
seeds, and all good products of the Sekhet
Hemat.   And this Sekhti journeyed to the
south unto Henenseten ; and when he came
to the lands of the house of Fefa, north of

Denat, he found a man there standing on the bank, a man called Hemti—the workman— son of a man called Asri, who was a serf of the High Steward Meruitensa. Now said this Hemti, when he saw the asses of Sekhti, that were pleasing in his eyes, " Oh that some good god would grant me to steal away the goods of Sekhti from him ! "

Now the Hemti's house was by the dyke of the tow-path, which was straitened, and not wide, as much as the width of a waist cloth : on the one side of it was the water, and on the other side of it grew his corn. Hemti said then to his servant, " Hasten ! bring me a shawl from the house," and it was brought instantly. Then spread he out this shawl on the face of the dyke, and it lay with its fastening on the water and its fringe on the corn.

Now Sekhti approached along the path used by all men. Said Hemti, " Have a care, Sekhti ! you are not going to trample on my clothes ! " Said Sekhti, " I will do

THE TRESPASS

as you like, I will pass carefully." Then
went he up on the higher side. But Hemti
said, "Go you over my corn, instead of the
path?" Said Sekhti, "I am going carefully;
this high field of corn is not my choice, but
you have stopped your path with your
clothes, and will you then not let us pass
by the side of the path?" And one of the
asses filled its mouth with a cluster of corn.
Said Hemti, "Look you, I shall take away
your ass, Sekhti, for eating my corn; behold
it will have to pay according to the amount
of the injury." Said Sekhti, "I am going
carefully; the one way is stopped, therefore
took I my ass by the enclosed ground, and
do you seize it for filling its mouth with a
cluster of corn? Moreover, I know unto
whom this domain belongs, even unto the
Lord Steward Meruitensa. He it is who
smites every robber in this whole land; and
shall I then be robbed in his domain?"

Said Hemti, "This is the proverb which
men speak : 'A poor man's name is only his

6

own matter.' I am he of whom you spake,
even the Lord Steward of whom you think."
Thereon he took to him branches of green
tamarisk and scourged all his limbs, took his
asses, and drave them into the pasture. And
Sekhti wept very greatly, by reason of the
pain of what he had suffered. Said Hemti,
"Lift not up your voice, Sekhti, or you
shall go to the Demon of Silence." Sekhti
answered, "You beat me, you steal my
goods, and now would take away even my
voice, O demon of silence! If you will
restore my goods, then will I cease to cry
out at your violence."

Sekhti stayed the whole day petitioning
Hemti, but he would not give ear unto him.
And Sekhti went his way to Khenensuten
to complain to the Lord Steward Meruitensa.
He found him coming out from the door of
his house to embark on his boat, that he
might go to the judgment hall. Sekhti said,
"Ho! turn, that I may please thy heart
with this discourse. Now at this time let

one of thy followers, whom thou wilt, come
to me that I may send
him to thee concerning
it." The Lord Steward
Meruitensa made his
follower, whom he
chose, go straight unto
him, and Sekhti sent
him back with an ac-
count of all
these mat-
ters. Then
the Lord
Steward

Meruitensa accused
Hemti unto the nobles
who sat with him; and
they said unto him, "By
your leave: As to this

Sekhti of yours, let him bring a witness.
Behold thou it is our custom with our
Sekhtis ; witnesses come with them ; behold,
that is our custom.   Then it will be fitting
to beat this Hemti for a trifle of natron and
a trifle of salt ; if he is commanded to pay
for it, he will pay for it."   But the High
Steward Meruitensa held his peace ; for he
would not reply unto these nobles, but
would reply unto the Sekhti.

Now Sekhti came to appeal to the Lord
Steward Meruitensa, and said, " O my Lord
Steward, greatest of the great, guide of the
needy :

When thou embarkest on the lake of truth,—
Mayest thou sail upon it with a fair wind ;
May thy mainsail not fly loose.
May there not be lamentation in thy cabin ;
May not misfortune come after thee.
May not thy mainstays be snapped ;
Mayest thou not run aground.
May not the wave seize thee ;
Mayest thou not taste the impurities of the river ;
Mayest thou not see the face of fear.

May the fish come to thee without escape ;
Mayest thou reach unto plump waterfowl.

For thou art the orphan's father, the widow's husband,
The desolate woman's brother, the garment of the
  motherless.

Let me celebrate thy name in this land for every
  virtue.
A guide without greediness of heart ;
A great one without any meanness.

Destroying deceit, encouraging justice ;
Coming to the cry, and allowing utterance.

Let me speak, do thou hear and do justice ;
O praised ! whom the praised ones praise.

Abolish oppression, behold me, I am overladen,
Reckon with me, behold me defrauded."

Now the Sekhti made this speech in the
time of the majesty of the King Neb-ka-n-ra,
blessed. The Lord Steward Meruitensa
went away straight to the king and said,
" My lord, I have found one of these Sekhti,
excellent of speech, in very truth ; stolen are
his goods, and he has come to complain to
me of the matter."

His majesty said, " As thou wishest that
I may see health ! lengthen out his complaint, without replying to any of his

speeches.   He who desireth him to continue
speaking should be silent ; behold, bring us
his words in writing, that we may listen to
them.   But provide for his wife and his
children, and let the Sekhti himself also have
a living.   Thou must cause one to give him
his portion without letting him know that
thou art he who is giving it to him.''

There were given to him four loaves and
two draughts of beer each day ; which the
Lord Steward Meruitensa provided for him,
giving it to a friend of his, who furnished it
unto him.   Then the Lord Steward Meruitensa sent the governor of the Sekhet Hemat
to make provision for the wife of the Sekhti,
three rations of corn each day.

Then came the Sekhti a second time, and
even a third time, unto the Lord Steward
Meruitensa ; but he told two of his followers
to go unto the Sekhti, and seize on him, and
beat him with staves.   But he came again
unto him, even unto six times, and said—

THE BEATING OF THE SEKHTI

" My Lord Steward—
Destroying deceit, and encouraging justice ;
Raising up every good thing, and crushing every evil ;
As plenty comes removing famine,
As clothing covers nakedness,
As clear sky after storm warms the shivering ;
As fire cooks that which is raw,
As water quenches the thirst ;
Look with thy face upon my lot; do not covet, but
  content me without fail ; do the right and do not
  evil."

But yet Meruitensa would not hearken unto his complaint; and the Sekhti came yet, and yet again, even unto the ninth time. Then the Lord Steward told two of his followers to go unto the Sekhti ; and the Sekhti feared that he should be beaten as at the third request. But the Lord Steward Meruitensa then said unto him, " Fear not, Sekhti, for what thou has done. The Sekhti has made many speeches, delightful to the heart of his majesty and I take an oath—as I eat bread, and as I drink water—that thou shalt be remembered to eternity." Said the Lord Steward, " Moreover, thou shalt be satis-

fied when thou shalt hear of thy complaints."
He caused to be written on a clean roll of
papyrus each petition to the end, and the
Lord Steward Meruitensa sent it to the
majesty of the King Neb-ka-n-ra, blessed,
and it was good to him more than anything
that is in the whole land : but his majesty
said to Meruitensa, " Judge it thyself ; I do
not desire it."

The Lord Steward Meruitensa made two
of his followers to go to the Sekhet Hemat,
and bring a list of the household of the
Sekhti ; and its amount was six persons,
beside his oxen and his goats, his wheat
and his barley, his asses and his dogs ; and
moreover he gave all that which belonged
unto the Hemti to the Sekhti, even all his
property and his offices, and the Sekhti was
beloved of the king more than all his over-
seers, and ate of all the good things of the
king, with all his household.

REMARKS

Of the tale of the peasant and the workman three copies, more or less imperfect,
remain to us. At Berlin are two papyri,
Nos. 2 and 4, containing parts of the tale,
published in fascimile in the " Denkmaler "
of Lepsius vi. 108–110 and 113 ; while
portions of another copy exist in the Butler
papyrus; and lately fragments of the same
have been collated in the collection of Lord
Amherst of Hackney.   These last have been
published in the Proceedings of the Society
of Biblical Archæology, xiv. 558.   The
number of copies seem to show that this was
a popular tale in early times ; it certainly is
of a more advanced type than the earlier tales
of magic, though it belongs to a simpler style
than the tales which follow.   It has been
translated partially by Chabas and Goodwin,
and also by Maspero, but most completely
by Griffith in the Proceedings of the Society
of Biblical Archæology, referred to above.

The beginning of the tale is lost in all the copies, and an introductory sentence is here added in brackets, to explain the position of affairs at the opening of the fragment. The essence of the tale is the difference in social position between the Sekhti, or peasant, and the Hemti, or workman—the *fellah* and the client of the noble ; and the impossibility of getting justice against a client, unless by some extraordinary means of attracting his patron's attention, is the basis of the action. There is not a single point of incident here which might not be true in modern times ; every turn of it seems to live, as one reads it in view of country life in Egypt.

The region of the tale is Henenseten, or Herakleopolis, now Ahnas, a little south of the Fayum. This was the seat of the IXth and Xth Dynasties, apparently ejected from Memphis by a foreign invasion of the Delta ; and here it is that the High Steward lives and goes to speak to the king. The district of the Sekhti is indicated by his travelling

south to Henenseten, and going with asses
and not by boat. Hence we are led to look
for the Sekhet Hemat, or salt country, in the
borders of the Fayum lake, whence the
journey would be southward, and across the
desert. This lake was not regulated artifici-
ally until the XIIth Dynasty; and hence at
the period of this tale it was a large sheet of
water, fluctuating with each rise and fall of
the Nile, and bordered by lagoons where
rushes would flourish, and where salt and
natron would accumulate during the dry
season of each year. At the present time the
lake of the Fayum is brackish, and the cliffs
which border it contain so much salt that rain
pools which collect on them are not drinkable.

The paths and roads of Egypt are not
protected by law as in Western countries.
Each person encroaches on a path or diverts
it as may suit his purpose, only checked by
the liberties taken by passers-by in trespassing
if a path be insufficient. Hence, it is very
usual to see a house built over half of a path,

and driving the traffic into the field or almost
over the river bank.   In this case the Hemti
had taken in as much of the path as he could,
and left it but a narrow strip along the top
of the canal bank.   The frequent use of the
public way for drying clothes, or spreading
out property, gave the idea of choking the
way altogether, and leaving no choice but
trespassing on the crops.   No sooner does a
donkey pause, or even pass, by a field of
corn than he snatches a mouthful, and in a
delay or altercation such as this the beast is
sure to take the advantage.   Donkeys carry-
ing loads by cornfields are usually muzzled
with rope nets, to prevent their feeding ; and
even sheep and goats are also fended in the
same way.

The proverb, " A poor man's name is only
his own matter," refers to the independent
fellah having no patron or protector who
will take up and defend his name from accu-
sations, as the interests of clients and serfs
would be protected.   This being the case,

Hemti therefore seizes on the property, and drives the asses into his own pasture field.

The scene of Meruitensa laying the case before the nobles who sat with him is interesting as showing that even simple cases were not decided by one judge, but referred to a council.   Similarly, Una lays stress on the private trial of the queen being confided to him and only one other judge.   Apparently, referring cases to a bench of judges was the means of preventing corruption.

The speeches of the Sekhti were given at full length in the papyrus, but owing to injuries we cannot now entirely recover them ; they are all in much the same strain, only the first and last are translated here, and the others are passed over.   The style of these speeches was evidently looked on as eloquent in those days, and this papyrus really seems to show the time when long-drawn comparisons and flowery wishes were in fashion.   It is far different from later compositions, as it is also from the earlier simple narration of crude marvels in the tales of the magicians.

The close of the tale is defective, but from the remains it appears to have ended by the gift of the Hemti's property to the oppressed Sekhti and the triumph of the injured peasant.

GOING TO WAWAT

XIITH DYNASTY

THE SHIPWRECKED SAILOR

THE wise servant said, " Let thy heart be satisfied, O my lord, for that we have come back to the country ; after we have long been on board, and rowed much, the prow has at last touched land. All the people rejoice, and embrace us one after another. Moreover, we have come back in good health, and not a man is lacking ; although we have been to the ends of Wawat, and gone through the land of Senmut, we have returned in peace, and our land—behold, we have come back to it. Hear me, my

7

lord; I have no other refuge. Wash thee, and turn the water over thy fingers; then go and tell the tale to the majesty."

His lord replied, " Thy heart continues still its wandering words! but although the mouth of a man may save him, his words may also cover his face with confusion. Wilt thou do then as thy heart moves thee? This that thou wilt say, tell quietly."

The sailor then answered, " Now I shall tell that which has happened to me, to my very self. I was going to the mines of Pharaoh, and I went down on the sea on a ship of 150 cubits long and 40 cubits wide, with 150 sailors of the best of Egypt, who had seen heaven and earth, and whose hearts were stronger than lions. They had said that the wind would not be contrary, or that there would be none. But as we approached the land the wind arose, and threw up waves eight cubits high. As for me, I seized a piece of wood ; but those who were in the vessel perished, without one remaining. A wave

threw me on an island, after that I had been
three days alone, without a companion beside
my own heart.   I laid me in a thicket, and
the shadow covered me.   Then stretched I my
limbs to try to find something for my mouth.
I found there figs and grapes, all manner of
good herbs, berries and grain, melons of all
kinds, fishes and birds.   Nothing was lacking.
And I satisfied myself ; and left on the
ground that which was over, of what my
arms had been filled withal.   I dug a pit,
I lighted a fire, and I made a burntoffering
unto the gods.

"Suddenly I heard a noise as of thunder,
which I thought to be that of a wave of the
sea.   The trees shook, and the earth was
moved.   I uncovered my face, and I saw that
a serpent drew near.   He was thirty cubits
long, and his beard greater than two cubits ;
his body was as overlayed with gold, and his
colour as that of true lazuli.   He coiled
himself before me.

" Then he opened his mouth, while that I

lay on my face before him, and he said to me,
'What has brought thee, what has brought
thee, little one, what has brought thee ?   If
thou sayest not speedily what has brought
thee to this isle, I will make thee know thyself; as a flame thou shalt vanish, if thou
tellest me not something I have not heard,
or which I knew not, before thee.'

"Then he took me in his mouth and
carried me to his resting-place, and layed
me down without any hurt.   I was whole
and sound, and nothing was gone from me.
Then he opened his mouth against me, while
that I lay on my face before him, and he
said, 'What has brought thee, what has
brought thee, little one, what has brought
thee to this isle which is in the sea, and of
which the shores are in the midst of the
waves ?'

"Then I replied to him, and holding my
arms low before him, I said to him, 'I was
embarked for the mines by the order of the
majesty, in a ship, 150 cubits was its length,

THE INQUIRY

and the width of it 40 cubits. It had 150
sailors of the best of Egypt, who had seen
heaven and earth, and the hearts of whom
were stronger than lions. They said that
the wind would not be contrary, or that
there would be none. Each of them ex-
ceeded his companion in the prudence of his
heart and the strength of his arm, and I was
not beneath any of them. A storm came upon
us while we were on the sea. Hardly could
we reach to the shore when the wind waxed yet
greater, and the waves rose even eight cubits.
As for me, I seized a piece of wood, while
those who were in the boat perished without
one being left with me for three days. Behold me now before thee, for I was brought
to this isle by a wave of the sea.'

" Then said he to me, ' Fear not, fear not,
little one, and make not thy face sad. If
thou hast come to me, it is God who has let
thee live. For it is He who has brought
thee to this isle of the blest, where nothing is
lacking, and which is filled with all good

things.   See now, thou shalt pass one month

after another, until thou shalt be four months in this isle.   Then a ship shall come from thy land with sailors, and thou shalt leave with them and go to thy country, and thou shalt die in thy town.

"'Con-verse is pleasing,

BRETHREN AND CHILDREN

and he who tastes of it passes over his misery.

I will therefore tell thee of that which is in this isle. I am here with my brethren and my children around me ; we are seventy-five serpents, children, and kindred ; without naming a young girl who was brought unto me by chance, and on whom the fire of heaven fell, and burnt her to ashes.

"'As for thee if thou art strong, and if thy heart waits patiently, thou shalt press thy infants to thy bosom and embrace thy wife. Thou shalt return to thy house which is full of all good things, thou shalt see thy land, where thou shalt dwell in the midst of thy kindred.'

"Then I bowed, in my obeisance, and I touched the ground before him. 'Behold now that which I have told thee before. I shall tell of thy presence unto Pharaoh, I shall make him to know of thy greatness, and I will bring to thee of the sacred oils and perfumes, and of incense of the temples with which all gods are honoured. I shall tell, moreover, of that which I do now see

(thanks to him), and there shall be rendered
to thee praises before the fulness of all the
land. I shall slay asses for thee in sacrifice, I
shall pluck for thee the birds, and I shall
bring for thee ships full of all kinds of the
treasures of Egypt, as is comely to do unto a
god, a friend of men in a far country, of
which men know not.'

" Then he smiled at my speech, because of
that which was in his heart, for he said to
me, ' Thou art not rich in perfumes, for all
that thou hast is but common incense. As
for me I am prince of the land of Punt, and
I have perfumes. Only the oil which thou
sayedst thou wouldest bring is not common in
this isle. But, when thou shalt depart from
this place, thou shalt never more see this isle ;
it shall be changed into waves.'

" And, behold, when the ship drew near,
according to all that he had told me before, I
got me up into an high tree, to strive to see
those who were within it. Then I came and
told to him this matter ; but it was already

known unto him before. Then he said to
me. 'Farewell, farewell, go to thy house,
little one, see again thy children, and let thy
name be good in thy town; these are my
wishes for thee.'

THE FAREWELL

"Then I bowed myself before him, and
held my arms low before him, and he, he
gave me gifts of precious perfumes, of cassia,
of sweet woods, of kohl, of cypress, an

abundance of incense, of ivory tusks, of baboons, of apes, and all kind of precious things. I embarked all in the ship which was come, and bowing myself, I prayed God for him.

"Then he said to me, 'Behold thou shalt come to thy country in two months, thou shalt press to thy bosom thy children, and thou shalt rest in thy tomb.' After this I went down to the shore unto the ship, and I called to the sailors who were there. Then on the shore I rendered adoration to the master of this isle and to those who dwelt therein.

"When we shall come, in our return, to the house of Pharaoh, in the second month, according to all that the serpent has said, we shall approach unto the palace. And I shall go in before Pharaoh, I shall bring the gifts which I have brought from this isle into the country. Then he shall thank me before the fulness of all the land. Grant then unto me a follower, and lead me to the courtiers of

the king. Cast thy eye upon me, after that
I am come to land again, after that I have
both seen and proved this. Hear my prayer,
for it is good to listen to people. It was
said unto me, ' Become a wise man, and thou
shalt come to honour,' and behold I have
become such."

This is finished from its beginning unto its
end, even as it was found in a writing. It is
written by the scribe of cunning fingers
Ameni-amen-aa ; may he live in life, wealth,
and health !

REMARKS

This tale is only known in one copy,
preserved in the Hermitage collection at
St. Petersburg. The papyrus has not yet
been published, either in facsimile or tran-
scription. But two translations of it have
appeared by M. Golénischeff : from the
earlier a modified translation is given by
Maspero in the " Contes Populaires," 2nd
edit., pp. 133–146, and the later translation is in M. Golénischeff's excellent

" Inventaire de la collection Egyptienne (Ermitage Impérial)," p. 177–182.

The tale is that of a returned sailor, speaking to his superior and telling his adventures, to induce him to send him on with an introduction to the king. At first his master professes to disbelieve him, and then the sailor protests that this happened to himself, and gives his narrative. The idea of an enchanted island, which has risen from the waves and will sink again, is here found to be one of the oldest plots for a tale of marvels. But the construction is far more advanced than that of the tales of the magicians. The family of serpents and the manner of the great serpent is well conceived, and there are many fine touches of literary quality : such as noise as of thunder, the trees shaking and the earth being moved at the appearance of the great serpent—the speeches of the serpent and his threat—the sailors who had seen heaven and earth—the contempt of the serpent for his offerings,

" As for me, I am prince of the land of
Punt, and I have perfumes "—and the scene
of departure. All of these points show a
firm hand and practised taste, although there
is still a style of simplicity clinging to it
which agrees well to its date in the XIIth
Dynasty.

The great serpent is not of a type usual
in Egyptian designs. The human-headed
uraeus is seldom bearded ; and the best
example of such a monster is on an
Ethiopian temple, where a great uraeus
has human arms and a lion's head. The
colours again repeat the favourite combina-
tion expressive of splendour — gold and
lazuli. Though lazuli is very rare in
early times, yet it certainly was known in
the XIIth Dynasty, as shown by the forms
of some beads of lazuli.

The slaughter of asses in sacrifice is a
very peculiar offering, and no sign of this
is found in any representations or groups of
offerings.

The colophon of the copyist at the end shows by the style of the name that it belongs to the earlier part of the XIIth Dynasty, and if so, the composition might be referred to the opening of foreign trade under Sankhkara or Amenemhat I.

XIIth DYNASTY

THE ADVENTURES OF SANEHAT

THE hereditary prince, royal seal-bearer, confidential friend, judge, keeper of the gate of the foreigners, true and beloved royal acquaintance, the royal follower Sanehat says :—

I attended my lord as a follower of the king, of the house of the hereditary princess, the greatly favoured, the royal wife, Ankhet-Usertesen, who shares the dwelling of the royal son Amenemhat in Kanefer.

In the thirtieth year, the month Paophi, the seventh day the god entered his horizon, the king Sehotepabra flew up to heaven and joined the sun's disc, the follower of the god

8

met his maker. The palace was silenced, and in mourning, the great gates were closed, the courtiers crouching on the ground, the people in hushed mourning.

His majesty had sent a great army with the nobles to the land of the Temehu (Lybia), his son and heir, the good god king Usertesen as their leader. Now he was returning, and had brought away living captives and all kinds of cattle without end. The councillors of the palace had sent to the West to let the king know the matter that had come to pass in the inner hall. The messenger was to meet him on the road, and reach him at the time of evening : the matter was urgent. "A hawk had soared with his followers." Thus said he, not to let the army know of it. Even if the royal sons who commanded in that army send a message, he was not to speak to a single one of them. But I was standing near, and heard his voice while he was speaking. I fled far away, my heart beating, my arms

failing, trembling had fallen on all my limbs.
I turned about in running to seek a place to
hide me, and I threw myself between two
bushes, to wait while they should pass by.

Tristram Ellis

THE FLIGHT

Then I turned me toward the south, not
from wishing to come into this palace—for
I knew not if war was declared—nor even
thinking a wish to live after this sovereign,

I turned my back to the sycamore, I reached Shi-Seneferu, and rested on the open field. In the morning I went on and overtook a man, who passed by the edge of the road. He asked of me mercy, for he feared me. By the evening I drew near to Kher-ahau (? old Cairo), and I crossed the river on a

THE CROSSING

raft without a rudder. Carried over by the west wind, I passed over to the east to the quarries of Aku and the land of the goddess Herit, mistress of the red mountain (Gebel Ahmar). Then I fled on foot, northward, and reached the walls of the prince, built to repel the Sati. I crouched in a bush

for fear of being seen by the guards, changed
each day, who watch on the top of the
fortress. I took my way by night, and at
the lighting of the day I reached Peten, and
turned me toward the valley of Kemur.
Then thirst hasted me on ; I dried up, and
my throat narrowed, and I said, " This is the

THE RESCUE

taste of death." When I lifted up my heart
and gathered strength, I heard a voice and
the lowing of cattle. I saw men of the Sati,
and one of them—a friend unto Egypt—
knew me. Behold he gave me water and
boiled me milk, and I went with him to his
camp ; they did me good, and one tribe
passed me on to another. I passed on

to Sun, and reached the land of Adim
(Edom).

When I had dwelt there half a year Amu-
an-shi—who is the prince of the Upper Tenu
—sent for me and said: "Dwell thou with me
that thou mayest hear the speech of Egypt."
He said thus for that he knew of my
excellence, and had heard tell of my worth,
for men of Egypt who were there with him
bore witness of me. Behold he said to me,
" For what cause hast thou come hither?
Has a matter come to pass in the palace?
Has the king of the two lands, Sehetep-
abra gone to heaven? That which has
happened about this is not known." But
I answered with concealment, and said,
" When I came from the land of the
Tamahu, and my desires were there changed
in me, if I fled away it was not by reason of
remorse that I took the way of a fugitive ; I
have not failed in my duty, my mouth has
not said any bitter words, I have not heard
any evil counsel, my name has not come into

the mouth of a magistrate. I know not by
what I have been led into this land." And
Amu-an-shi said, " This is by the will of the
god (king of Egypt), for what is a land like
if it know not that excellent god, of whom
the dread is upon the lands of strangers,
as they dread Sekhet in a year of pestilence."
I spake to him, and replied, " Forgive me,
his son now enters the palace, and has received the heritage of his father. He is a god
who has none like him, and there is none
before him. He is a master of wisdom,
prudent in his designs, excellent in his
decrees, with good-will to him who goes or
who comes ; he subdued the land of strangers
while his father yet lived in his palace, and
he rendered account of that which his father
destined him to perform. He is a brave
man, who verily strikes with his sword ; a
valiant one, who has not his equal ; he
springs upon the barbarians, and throws
himself on the spoilers ; he breaks the horns
and weakens the hands, and those whom he

smites cannot raise the buckler. He is fearless, and dashes the heads, and none can stand before him. He is swift of foot, to destroy him who flies ; and none who flees from him reaches his home. His heart is strong in his time ; he is a lion who strikes with the claw, and never has he turned his back. His heart is closed to pity ; and when he sees multitudes, he leaves none to live behind him. He is a valiant one who springs in front when he sees resistance ; he is a warrior who rejoices when he flies on the barbarians. He seizes the buckler, he rushes forward, he never needs to strike again, he slays and none can turn his lance ; and when he takes the bow the barbarians flee from his arms like dogs ; for the great goddess has given to him to strike those who know her not ; and if he reaches forth he spares none, and leaves nought behind. He is a friend of great sweetness, who knows how to gain love ; his land loves him more than itself, and rejoices in him more than in its own

god ; men and women run to his call. A
king, he has ruled from his birth ; he, from
his birth, has increased births, a sole being, a
divine essence, by whom this land rejoices to
be governed. He enlarges the borders of
the South ; but he covets not the lands of
the North : he does not smite the Sati, nor
crush the Nemau-shau. If he descends here,
let him know thy name, by the homage
which thou wilt pay to his majesty. For he
refuses not to bless the land which obeys
him."

And he replied to me, " Egypt is
indeed happy and well settled ; behold
thou art far from it, but whilst thou art
with me I will do good unto thee." And
he placed me before his children, he mar-
ried his eldest daughter to me, and gave
me the choice of all his land, even among
the best of that which he had on the border
of the next land. It is a goodly land, Iaa
is its name. There are figs and grapes ;
there is wine commoner than water ; abun-

dant is the honey, many are its olives ; and all fruits are upon its trees ; there is barley and wheat, and cattle of kinds without end. This was truly a great thing that he granted me, when the prince came to invest me, and

SANEHAT MEETING THE TENU

establish me as prince of a tribe in the best of his land. I had my continual portion of bread and of wine each day, of cooked meat, of roasted fowl, as well as the wild game which I took, or which was brought to me,

besides what my dogs captured. They made
me much butter, and prepared milk of all
kinds. I passed many years, the children
that I had became great, each ruling his tribe.
When a messenger went or came to the
palace, he turned aside from the way to come
to me ; for I helped every man. I gave
water to the thirsty, I set on his way him
who went astray, and I rescued the robbed.
The Sati who went far, to strike and turn
back the princes of other lands, I ordained
their goings ; for the Prince of the Tenu for
many years appointed me to be general of his
soldiers. In every land which I attacked I
played the champion, I took the cattle, I led
away the vassals, I carried off the slaves, I
slew the people, by my sword, my bow, my
marches and my good devices. I was
excellent to the heart of my prince ; he
loved me when he knew my power, and set
me over his children when he saw the
strength of my arms.

A champion of the Tenu came to defy

me in my tent : a bold man without equal,
for he had vanquished the whole country.
He said, "Let Sanehat fight with me ;" for
he desired to overthrow me, he thought to
take my cattle for his tribe. The prince
councilled with me. I said, "I know him
not. I certainly am not of his degree, I
hold me far from his place. Have I ever
opened his door, or leaped over his fence?
It is some envious jealousy from seeing me ;
does he think that I am like some steer
among the cows, whom the bull overthrows?
If this is a wretch who thinks to enrich himself at my cost, not a Bedawi and a Bedawi
fit for fight, then let us put the matter to
judgment. Verily a true bull loves battle,
but a vain-glorious bull turns his back for
fear of contest ; if he has a heart for combat,
let him speak what he pleases. Will God
forget what He has ordained, and how shall
that be known ?" I lay down ; and when
I had rested I strung my bow, I made ready
my arrows, I loosened my poignard, I

furbished my arms. At dawn the land of
the Tenu came together ; it had gathered
its tribes and called all the neighbouring
people, it spake of nothing but the fight.
Each heart burnt for me, men and women
crying out; for each heart was troubled for

THE COMBAT

me, and they said, " Is there another strong
one who would fight with him ? Behold the
adversary has a buckler, a battle axe, and an
armful of javelins." Then I drew him to
the attack ; I turned aside his arrows, and
they struck the ground in vain. One drew

near to the other, and he fell on me, and
then I shot him. My arrow fastened in his
neck, he cried out, and fell on his face : I
drove his lance into him, and raised my
shout of victory on his back. Whilst all
the men of the land rejoiced, I, and his
vassals whom he had oppressed, gave thanks
unto Mentu. This prince, Amu-an-shi,
embraced me. Then I carried off his goods
and took his cattle, that which he had wished
to do to me, I did even so unto him ; I
seized that which was in his tent, I spoiled
his dwelling. As time went on I increased
the richness of my treasures and the number
of my cattle.

Petition to the king of Egypt.

" Now behold what the god has done for
me who trusted in him. Having once fled
away, yet now there is a witness of me in
the palace. Once having fled away, as a
fugitive,——now all in the palace give unto
me a good name. After that I had been

dying of hunger, now I give bread to those around. I had left my land naked, and now I am clothed in fine linen. After having been a wanderer without followers, now I possess many serfs. My house is fine, my land wide, my memory is established in the temple of all the gods. And let this flight obtain thy forgiveness; that I may be appointed in the palace; that I may see the place where my heart dwells. How great a thing is it that my body should be embalmed in the land where I was born! To return there is happiness. I have made offering to God to grant me this thing. His heart suffers who has run away unto a strange land. Let him hear the prayer of him who is afar off, that he may revisit the place of his birth, and the place from which he removed.

" May the king of Egypt be gracious to me that I may live of his favour. And I render my homage to the mistress of the land, who is in his palace; may I hear the news of her

children. Thus will my limbs grow young
again. Now old age comes, feebleness
seizes me, my eyes are heavy, my arms are
feeble, my legs will not move, my heart is
slow. Death draws nigh to me, soon shall
they lead me to the city of eternity. Let
me follow the mistress of all (the queen, his
former mistress) ; lo ! let her tell me the
excellencies of her children ; may she bring
eternity to me."

Then the majesty of King Kheper-ka-ra,
the blessed, spake upon this my desire that
I had made to him. His majesty sent unto
me with presents from the king, that he
might enlarge the heart of his servant, like
unto the province of any strange land ; and
the royal sons who are in the palace addressed
themselves unto me.

Copy of the decree which was brought—to
me who speak to you—to lead me back
into Egypt.

"The Horus, life of births, lord of the

crowns, life of births, king of Upper and
Lower Egypt, Kheper-ka-ra, son of the Sun,
Amen-em-hat, ever living unto eternity.
Order for the follower Sanehat. Behold this
order of the king is sent to thee to instruct
thee of his will.

EGYPTIAN MESSENGERS ARRIVING

Now, although thou hast gone through
strange lands from Adim to Tenu, and
passed from one country to another at the
wish of thy heart — behold, what hast thou
done, or what has been done against thee,
that is amiss? Moreover, thou reviledst not;

9

but if thy word was denied, thou didst not speak again in the assembly of the nobles, even if thou wast desired. Now, therefore, that thou hast thought on this matter which has come to thy mind, let thy heart not change again ; for this thy Heaven (queen), who is in the palace is fixed, she is flourishing, she is enjoying the best in the kingdom of the land, and her children are in the chambers of the palace.

" Leave all the riches that thou hast, and that are with thee, altogether. When thou shalt come into Egypt behold the palace, and when thou shalt enter the palace, bow thy face to the ground before the Great House ; thou shalt be chief among the companions. And day by day behold thou growest old ; thy vigour is lost, and thou thinkest on the day of burial. Thou shalt see thyself come to the blessed state, they shall give thee the bandages from the hand of Tait, the night of applying the oil of embalming. They shall follow thy funeral,

and visit the tomb on the day of burial,
which shall be in a gilded case, the head
painted with blue, a canopy of cypress wood
above thee, and oxen shall draw thee, the
singers going before thee, and they shall
dance the funeral dance. The weepers
crouching at the door of thy tomb shall
cry aloud the prayers for offerings : they
shall slay victims for thee at the door of
thy pit ; and thy pyramid shall be carved
in white stone, in the company of the royal
children. Thus thou shalt not die in a
strange land, nor be buried by the Amu ;
thou shalt not be laid in a sheep-skin when
thou art buried ; all people shall beat the
earth, and lament on thy body when thou
goest to the tomb."

When this order came to me, I was in
the midst of my tribe. When it was read
unto me, I threw me on the dust, I threw
dust in my hair ; I went around my tent

rejoicing and saying, "How may it be that such a thing is done to the servant, who with a rebellious heart has fled to strange lands? Now with an excellent deliverance, and mercy dèlivering me from death, thou shall cause me to end my days in the palace."

Copy of the answer to this order.

"The follower Sanehat says : In excellent peace above everything consider of this flight that he made here in his ignorance ; Thou, the Good God, Lord of both Lands, Loved of Ra, Favourite of Mentu, the lord of Thebes, and of Amen, lord of thrones of the lands, of Sebek, Ra, Horus, Hathor, Atmu, and of his fellow-gods, of Sopdu, Neferbiu, Samsetu, Horus, lord of the east, and of the royal uraeus which rules on thy head, of the chief gods of the waters, of Min, Horus of the desert, Urrit, mistress of Punt, Nut, Harnekht, Ra, all the gods of the land of Egypt, and of the isles of the sea. May they give life and peace to

thy nostril, may they load thee with their
gifts, may they give to thee eternity without
end, everlastingness without bound. May
the fear of thee be doubled in the lands of
the deserts. Mayest thou subdue the circuit
of the sun's disc. This is the prayer to his
master of the humble servant who is saved
from a foreign land.

"O wise king, the wise words which
are pronounced in the wisdom of the majesty
of the sovereign, thy humble servant fears
to tell. It is a great thing to repeat. O
great God, like unto Ra in fulfilling that
to which he has set his hand, what am I
that he should take thought for me? Am
I among those whom he regards, and for
whom he arranges? Thy majesty is as
Horus, and the strength of thy arms extends
to all lands.

"Then let his Majesty bring Maki of
Adma, Kenti-au-ush of Khenti-keshu, and
Tenus from the two lands of the Fenkhu;
these are the princes who bear witness of

me as to all that has passed, out of love for thyself. Does not Tenu believe that it belongs to thee like thy dogs. Behold this flight that I have made : I did not have it in my heart ; it was like the leading of a dream, as a man of Adehi (Delta) sees himself in Abu (Elephantine), as a man of the plain of Egypt who sees himself in the deserts. There was no fear, there was no hastening after me, I did not listen to an evil plot, my name was not heard in the mouth of the magistrate ; but my limbs went, my feet wandered, my heart drew me ; my god commanded this flight, and drew me on ; but I am not stiff-necked. Does a man fear when he sees his own land ? Ra spread thy fear over the land, thy terrors in every strange land. Behold me now in the palace, behold me in this place ; and lo ! thou art he who is over all the horizon ; the sun rises at thy pleasure, the water in the rivers is drunk at thy will, the wind in heaven is breathed at thy saying.

"I who speak to thee shall leave my goods to the generations to follow in this land. And as to this messenger who is come even let thy majesty do as pleaseth him, for one lives by the breath that thou givest. O thou who art beloved of Ra, of Horus, and of Hathor; Mentu, lord of Thebes, desires that thy august nostril should live for ever."

I made a feast in Iaa, to pass over my goods to my children. My eldest son was leading my tribe, all my goods passed to him, and I gave him my corn and all my cattle, my fruit, and all my pleasant trees. When I had taken my road to the south, and arrived at the roads of Horus, the officer who was over the garrison sent a messenger to the palace to give notice. His majesty sent the good overseer of the peasants of the king's domains, and boats laden with presents from the king for the Sati who

had come to conduct me to the roads of
Horus. I spoke to each one by his name,
and I gave the presents to each as was
intended. I received and I returned the
salutation, and I continued thus until I
reached the city of Thetu.

When the land was brightened, and the
new day began, four men came with a
summons for me; and the four men went
to lead me to the palace. I saluted with
both my hands on the ground; the royal
children stood at the courtyard to conduct
me: the courtiers who were to lead me to
the hall brought me on the way to the
royal chamber.

I found his Majesty on the great throne
in the hall of pale gold. Then I threw
myself on my belly; this god, in whose
presence I was, knew me not. He
questioned me graciously, but I was as
one seized with blindness, my spirit fainted,
my limbs failed, my heart was no longer
in my bosom, and I knew the difference

between life and death. His majesty said
to one of the companions, "Lift him up,
let him speak to me." And his majesty
said, "Behold thou hast come, thou hast
trodden the deserts, thou hast played the
wanderer. Decay falls on thee, old age
has reached thee; it is no small thing that
thy body should be embalmed, that the
Pedtiu shall not bury thee. Do not, do
not, be silent and speechless; tell thy
name; is it fear that prevents thee?" I
answered in reply, "I fear, what is it that
my lord has said that I should answer it?
I have not called on me the hand of God,
but it is terror in my body, like that which
brings sudden death. Now behold I am
before thee; thou art life; let thy majesty
do what pleaseth him."

The royal children were brought in, and
his majesty said to the queen, "Behold thou
Sanehat has come as an Amu, whom the
Sati have produced."

She cried aloud, and the royal children

spake with one voice, saying, before his
majesty, " Verily it is not so, O king, my
lord." Said his majesty, " It is verily he."
Then they brought their collars, and their
wands, and their sistra in their hands, and
displayed them before his majesty; and they
sang—

" May thy hands prosper, O king ;
May the ornaments of the Lady of Heaven continue.
May the goddess Nub give life to thy nostril ;
May the mistress of the stars favour thee, when thou
    sailest south and north.
All wisdom is in the mouth of thy majesty;
Thy uraeus is on thy forehead, thou drivest away
    the miserable.
Thou art pacified, O Ra, lord of the lands ;
They call on thee as on the mistress of all.
        Strong is thy horn,
        Thou lettest fly thine arrow.
Grant the breath to him who is without it ;
Grant good things to this traveller, Samehit the Pedti,
    born in the land of Egypt,
Who fled away from fear of thee,
And fled this land from thy terrors.
Does not the face grow pale, of him who beholds thy
    countenance ;
Does not the eye fear, which looks upon thee.'

THE SONG OF THE PRINCESSES

Said his majesty, " Let him not fear, let him be freed from terror. He shall be a Royal Friend amongst the nobles ; he shall be put within the circle of the courtiers. Go ye to the chamber of praise to seek wealth for him."

When I went out from the palace, the royal children offered their hands to me ; we walked afterwards to the Great Gates. I was placed in a house of a king's son, in which were delicate things, a place of coolness, fruits of the granary, treasures of the White House, clothes of the king's guardrobe, frankincense, the finest perfumes of the king and the nobles whom he loves, in every chamber. All the servitors were in their several offices.

Years were removed from my limbs : I was shaved, and polled my locks of hair ; the foulness was cast to the desert with the garments of the Nemau-sha. I clothed me in fine linen, and anointed myself with the fine oil of Egypt ; I laid me on a bed. I gave up the sand to those who lie on it ; the oil of wood to him who would anoint himself therewith. There was given to me the mansion of a lord of serfs, which had belonged to a royal friend. There many ex-

THE SHAVING OF SANEHAT

cellent things were in its buildings; all its wood was renewed. There were brought to me portions from the palace, thrice and four times each day ; besides the gifts of the royal children, always, without ceasing. There was built for me a pyramid of stone

amongst the pyramids. The overseer of the
architects measured its ground ; the chief
treasurer wrote it ; the sacred masons cut the
well ; the chief of the labourers on the tombs
brought the bricks; all things used to make
strong a building were there used. There
were given to me peasants ; there were made
for me a garden, and fields in it before my
mansion, as is done for the chief royal friend.
My statue was inlayed with gold, its girdle of
pale gold ; his majesty caused it to be made.
Such is not done to a man of low degree.

May I be in the favour of the king until
the day shall come of my death.

(*This is finished from beginning to end, as
was found in the writing.*)

REMARKS

The Adventures of Sanehat appears to
have been a popular tale, as portions of
three copies remain. The first papyrus

known (Berlin No. 1) was imperfect at the
beginning ; but since then a flake of lime-
stone found in a tomb bore the beginning
of the tale, and the same part is found on
a papyrus in the Amherst collection. The
main text has been translated by Chabas
("Le papyrus de Berlin," 37–51), Goodwin,
and Maspero ("Mel. d'arch.," iii. 68, 140,
and "Contes Populaire," 89–130) ; while
the beginning is treated in "Mémoires de
l'institut Egyptien," ii. 1–23, and in Proc.
S.B.A., 452. The present translation is
mainly based on Mr. Griffith's readings in
all cases of difficulty.

This is perhaps the most interesting of all
the tales, because it bears such signs of being
written in the times of which it treats, it
throws so much light on the life of the time
in Egypt and Syria, and if not a real narrative, it is at least so probable that it may be
accepted without much difficulty. For my
own part, I incline to look on it as strictly
historical ; and in the absence of a single

point of doubt, I shall here treat it as seriously
as the biographical inscriptions of the early
tombs.   Possibly some day the tomb of
Sanehat may be found, and the whole
inscription be read complete upon the
walls.

The name Sa-nehat means " son of the
sycamore," probably from his having been
born, or living, at some place where was a
celebrated sacred sycamore. This was a
common tree in ancient, as in modern,
Egypt ; but an allusion in the tale, to Sanehat
turning his back on the sycamore, when he
was fleeing apparently up the west side of the
Delta, makes it probable that the sycamore
was that of Aa-tenen, now Batnun, at the
middle of the west side of the Delta.

The titles given to Sanehat at the opening
are of a very high rank, and imply that he
was the son either of the king or of a great
noble.   And his position in the queen's
household shows him to have been of im-
portance ; the manner in which he is received

by the royal family at the end implying that he was quite familiar with them in early days.

But the great difficulty in the account has been the sudden panic of Sanehat on hearing of the death of Amenemhat, and no explanation of this has yet been brought forward. It seems not unlikely that he was a son of Amenemhat by some concubine. This would at once account for his high titles—for his belonging to the royal household—for his fear of his elder brother Usertesen, who might see in him a rival, and try to slay him after his father's death—for the command to him to leave all his possessions and family behind him in Syria, as the condition of his being allowed to return to end his days in Egypt—for his familiar reception by the royal family, and for the property given to him on his return.

The date recorded for the death of Sehotepabra—Amenemhat I., the founder of the XIIth Dynasty—agrees with the limit of his reign on the monuments. And the expres-

sions for his death are valuable as showing
the manner in which a king's decease was
regarded ; under the emblem of a hawk—the
bird of Ra—he flew up and joined the sun.

Sometime before his death Amenemhat
had been in retirement ; after twenty years
of reign (which was probably rather late in
his life, as he seems to have forced his way to
the front as a successful man and founder of
a family) he had associated his son, the first
Usertesen, on the throne, and apparently
resigned active life ; for in the third year of
Usertesen we find the coregent summoning
his court and decreeing the founding of the
temple of Heliopolis without any mention
of his father. The old king, however, lived
yet ten years after his retirement, and died
(as this narrative shows us) during an expedi-
tion of his son Usertesen.

The time of year mentioned here would
fall in about the middle of the inundation in
those days. Hence it seems that the military
expeditions were made after the harvest was

secured, and while the country was under water and the population disengaged from other labour.

The course of Sanehat's flight southward, reaching the Nile at Cairo after two days' haste, indicates that the army was somewhere west of the Delta. This would point to its being on the road to the oasis of the Natron Lakes, which would be the natural course for a body of men needing water supply. His throwing himself between two bushes to hide from the army shows that the message came early in the day, otherwise he would have fled in the dark. He then fled a day's journey to the south, turning his back on the sycamore, and slept in the open field at Shi-Seneferu somewhere below the Barrage. The second day he reached the Nile opposite Old Cairo in the afternoon, and ferried himself over, passed the quarries at Gebel Mokattam, and the red hill of Gebel Ahmar, and came to a frontier wall before dark. This cannot have been far from Old Cairo, by the time ;

and as Heliopolis was in course of building by Usertesen, it would be probably on the desert near there, for the protection of the town. Passing the desert guards by night he pushed on and reached Peten, near Belbeis, by dawn, and turned east toward the valley of Kemur, or Wady Tumilat. Here in his extremity he was found by the Sati or Asiatics, and rescued. This shows that the eastern desert was left to the wandering tribes, and was without any regular government at this period; though all the eastern Delta was already well in Egyptian hands, as we know by the monuments at Bubastis, Dedamun, and Tanis.

The land of Adim to which Sanehat fled appears to be the same as Edom or the southeast corner of Syria. It was evidently near the upper Tenu, or Rutennu, who seem to have dwelt on the hill country of Palestine. The hill and the plain of Palestine are so markedly different, that in all ages they have tended to be held by opposing people. In

the time of Sanehat the upper Tenu who held
the hills were opposed to the Tenu in general
who held the plains ; later on the Semites of
the hills opposed the Philistines of the plain,
and now the *fellah* of the hills opposes
the Bedawi of the plain. The district of
Amuanshi in which Sanehat settled was a
goodly land, bearing figs and grapes and
olives, flowing with wine and honey and oil,
yielding barley and wheat without end, and
much cattle. This abundance points rather
to the hill country near Hebron or between
there and Beit Jibrin, as this south part of
the hills is notably fertile. The Tenu who
came to defy Sanehat, being in opposition to
the upper Tenu, were probably those of the
plain ; and the opposition to Sanehat may
have arisen from his encroaching on the
fertile plain at the foot of his hills, as he
was in the best of the land " on the border
of the next land."

The Egyptian was evidently looked on as
being of a superior race by the Tenu, and

his civilisation won for him the confidence which many wandering Englishmen now find in Africa or Polynesia, like John Dunn. The set combat of two champions seems—by the large gathering—to have been a well-recognised custom among the Tenu, while it exactly accords with Goliath's offer in later times. And raising the shout of victory on the back of the fallen champion reminds us of David's standing on Goliath.

The transition from the recital of the Syrian adventures to the petition to Pharaoh is not marked in the manuscript ; but from the construction the beginning of the petition is evidently at the place here marked. The manner in which Sanehat appeals to the queen shows how well he must have been known to her in his former days.

The decree in reply to Sanehat is in the regular style of royal decrees of the period. Apparently by a clerical error the scribe has substituted the name Amenemhat for Usertesen, but the Horus name and the throne name

leave no doubt that Usertesen I. is intended
here. The tone of the reply is as gracious
as possible, according with the king's character as stated by Sanehat, " He is a friend
of great sweetness, and knows how to gain
love." He quite recognises the inquiries
after the queen, and replies concerning her.
And then he assures Sanehat of welcome on
his return, and promises him all that he asks,
including a tomb " in the company of the
royal children," a full recognition of his
real rank. Incidentally we learn that the
Amu buried their dead wrapped in a sheep's
skin ; as we also learn, further on, that they
anointed themselves with oil (olive ?), wore
the hair long, and slept on the ground.

The funeral that is promised accords with
the burials of the XIIth Dynasty : the
gilded case, the head painted blue, and the
canopy of cypress wood, are all known of
this period, but would be out of place in
describing a Ramesside burial.

Sanehat's reply is a full course of the usual

religious adulation, and differs in this remark-
ably from his petition. In fact it is hard to
be certain where his petition begins ; possibly
the opening of it has been lost out of the
text in copying from a mutilated papyrus ; or
possibly it was sent merely as a memorandum
of Sanehat's position and desires, without ven-
turing to address it personally to the king ;
or even it may have not been allowable then
to make such petitions formally, so as to
leave the initiative to the king's free will,
just as it is not allowable nowadays to
question royalty, but only to answer when
spoken to.

The proposal to bring forward his fellow-
sheikhs as witnesses of his unabated loyalty
is very curious, and seems superfluous after
Usertesen's assurances. Beyond Abisha of
the Amu at Beni Hasan, these are the only
early personal names of Syrians that we
know. The Fenkhu in this connection can
hardly be other than the Phœnicians ; and, if
so, this points to their being already estab-

lished in southern Syria at this date. But these chiefs were not allowed to come forward ; and it seems to have been the policy of Egypt to keep the Syrians off as much as possible, not a single man who came with Sanehat being allowed to cross the frontier. The allusion to the Tenu belonging to Pharaoh, like his dogs, is peculiarly fitting to this period, as the dog seems to have been more familiarly domesticated in the XIth and XIIth Dynasties than at any other age, and dogs are often then represented on the funereal steles, even with their names.

The expression for strangeness—"as a man of the Delta sees himself at the cataract, as a man of the plain who sees himself in the deserts"—is true to this day. Nothing upsets an Egyptian's self-reliance like going back a few miles into the desert ; and almost any man of the cultivated plain will flee with terror if he finds himself left alone far in the desert, or even taken to the top of the desert hills.

We learn incidentally that the Egyptian frontier, even in the later years of Usertesen I., had not been pushed beyond the Wady Tumilat ; for Sanehat travels south to the Roads of Horus, where he finds the frontier garrison, and leaves his Syrian friends; and there laden boats meet him, showing that it must have been somewhere along a waterway from the Nile.

The abasement of Sanehat might well be due to natural causes, beside the reverence for the divine person of the king. The Egyptian court must have seemed oppressively splendid, with the brilliant and costly workmanship of Usertesen, to one who had lived a half-wild life for so many years ; and, more than that, the recalling of all his early days and habits and friendships would overwhelm his mind and make it difficult to collect his thoughts.

Sanehat's appearance was so much changed by his long hair, his age, and his strange dress, that his former mistress and com-

panions could not recognise him. The use
of collars and sceptres in the song and dance
is not clear to us. The sistra were, of course,
to beat or rattle in time with the song; the
sceptres or wands were perhaps the same as
the engraved wands of ivory common in the
XIIth Dynasty, or of blue glazed ware in
XVIIIth, and would be used to wave or beat
time with; but the use of the collar and
counterpoise, or *menat*, is unexplained, though
figures of dancers are shown holding a collar
and *menat*, and such objects were found
buried in the ceremonial foundation deposit
of Tahutmes III. at Koptos.

This song of the princesses is clearly in
parallel phrases. First are four wishes for
the king and queen, in four lines. Second,
an ascription of wisdom and power, in two
lines. Third, a comparison of the king to
Ra, and of the queen to the great goddess, in
two lines. Fourth, an ascription of fighting
power. Fifth, a petition for Sanehat, wind-
ing up with the statement of fear inspired by

the king, as explaining Sanehat's abasement.
To this the king responds by reassuring
Sanehat, and promising him position and
wealth.

The account of Sanehat's renewal of his
old national ways can best be appreciated by
any one who has lived a rough life for a time
and then comes back to civilisation.   Doubtless these comforts were all the more grateful
to him in his old age, when he was weary of
his unsettled life.

In the preparation of his tomb it is stated
to have been a pyramid, with rock-cut well
chamber, and built of bricks above.   This
just accords with the construction of the
pyramids of the XIIth Dynasty.

The last phrase implies that this was com-
posed during Sanehat's life ; and such a life
would be so remarkable that this biography
might be prepared with good reason.   Also
it is very unlikely that a mere story-teller
would have dropped the relation without
describing his grand funeral which was pro-

mised to him. From suddenly stopping at the preparation of the tomb, without going further, we have a strong presumption that this was a true narrative, written at Sanehat's dictation, and probably intended to be inscribed on his tomb wall. In any case, we have here an invaluable picture of life in Palestine and in Egypt, and the relations of the two countries, at an epoch before the time of Abraham, and not paralleled by any other document until more than a thousand years later.

INDEX

—◆◇◆—

www.ingramcontent.com/pod-product-compliance
Lightning Source LLC
LaVergne TN
LVHW091301080426
835510LV00007B/350